Journey
to Your Heart Space

A mandala coloring book
to illuminate a gentle
forgiveness process

11 Illuminations • 11 Coloring Mandalas
22 Journaling Pages

Brenda Reiss

Journey to Your Heart Space: A Mandala Coloring Book to Illuminate the Path From Your Head to Your Heart

Limits of Liability and Disclaimer of Warranty

The author/publisher shall not be liable for your misuse of this material. This book is strictly for informational and educational purposes.

Warning - Disclaimer

The purpose of this book is to educate and entertain. It is distributed with the understanding that the publisher is not engaged in the dispensation of legal, psychological or any other professional advice. The content of each entry is the expression and opinion of its author and does not necessarily reflect the beliefs, practices or viewpoints of the publisher, its parent company or its affiliates. The publisher's choice to include any material within is not intended to express or imply any warranties or guarantees of any kind. The author and/or publisher do not guarantee that anyone following these techniques, suggestions, tips, ideas, or strategies will become successful. The author and/or publisher shall have neither liability nor responsibility to anyone with respect to any loss or damage caused, or alleged to be caused, directly or indirectly by the information contained in this book.

Table of Contents

A Gentle Path From Your Head to Your Heart

What a joy it is to share *Journey to Your Heart Space* with you.

When I first heard that the longest journey is the distance from your head to your heart, I didn't know what it meant. See, I spent most of my life living in the so-called safety of making decisions from my head and protecting my heart. I didn't realize that it didn't feel safe for me to trust my heart due to life situations and circumstances that affected me deeply.

As I journeyed through a beautiful process of forgiveness through steps that have been illuminated in this book, my life started changing, and that journey started happening organically to where I love being in my heart space. Creating the balance of living from my heart and head continues to be a journey of love and an every day experience.

That's why I am honored to collaborate with Michelle Radomski who has created these gorgeous "intention-infused" coloring mandalas. The steps are powerful and provide a path for deeper reflection of your life journey. Adding the mandalas to this beautiful process, provides a way to quiet the mind so that your heart space can open and amazing revelations can be revealed.

Forgiveness is not just about releasing resentment and anger; forgiveness is about cultivating an environment of acceptance and allowance so that you can create the life you are destined to live.

I'd love to hear about our experiences. Please reach out to me through Brendareisscoaching.com

With so much love and gratitude,

Brenda

Meeting the Mandalas

I believe that the work of our heart often finds us through the most curious circumstances. That's how I met the mandalas.

Seven years ago I "just happened" to receive an unsolicited email from a mandala artist offering 15 coloring mandalas. For free! I quickly said yes, and downloaded the pages. I bought a brand new box of 64 crayons, started coloring, and was completely, gloriously, swept away. Mandalas had my heart.

Shortly after that I experienced a small set back in my business. I needed another stream of income. "Mandalas," I heard. "Create mandalas."

"Wait … what,?" I thought. Then, in a flash, I "just happened" to remember a friend who made personalized fractal mandalas. He had only been doing it a few months and his success was rapidly growing. I whispered another, "yes," and the mandalas entered my business.

I had zero idea how to even begin, so I hit the Internet. After hours of exploring I saw this: **"Sometimes I use words in my mandalas."**

That was it! The magic moment when grace arrives and everything falls into place.

I love words—meaningful words, powerful words, uplifting and inspiring words. I sat at my computer and typed in the word "Love." Then I played with the shapes I saw in the letters. I duplicated them, intertwined them, flipped them, and flopped them. In the end I had my very first Coloring Mandala … created (literally) from "Love."

Mandala in Sanskrit means, "circle, or container of sacred essence." When I create my mandalas, I (consciously and mindfully) focus on the energy of the word I am using and then place it into the mandala. So when you interact and engage with the mandala through the process of coloring, you are saying. "Yes!" to the energy it holds. You are working with the sacred essence of that word, held in the container of the mandala.

The mandalas have much to teach you. They can quiet your mind when it is raging, soothe your soul when it is hurting, and provide inspiration when you are seeking. I invite you to ground and center yourself, and then connect with your very own version of "deeper truth" before you begin to color. Hold a question, a desire, or a dream in your mind. Begin to color, and trust that inspiration will come. The mandalas will meet you where you are, and gently guide you to where you wish to be.

My wish is that your heart will be touched with the power of forgiveness as you focus on Brenda's illuminations, color the mandalas, and then journal about your insights and "aha" moments.

To meaningful words and glorious color!

Michelle

I Am Opening

Sometimes the heart feels closed and heavy

I become willing to explore the heavy

In the exploring, I feel some lightness

As I follow this light, it gets brighter

I sit in the space of light and dark

And I take a breath with ease

Being open-minded about exploring the process of forgiveness is key to finding a way to make it work in your life. Those who remain closed to the idea have a much more difficult time of moving on.

I Am Opening

I Am Opening

I Am Opening

I Am Curious

Curiosity opens me to the wonders of life.

Approaching each day with a curious

mind helps me feel safe

AND open to taking steps

toward unfolding possibility.

Curiosity is innate in all of us. That's how creations are born. We explore, investigate and learn more about ourselves and each other. As we allow ourselves to be curious, it opens up pathways to new ideas and ways of being.

I Am Curious

I Am Curious

I Am Curious

I Am Aware

I look around with an open mind

and an awakening heart to all

that is emerging around me.

I become aware of the colors, textures,

and subtleties that shape my life.

Having an awareness of yourself and what role you play in your life situations is important to finding forgiveness. It's not a case of blaming or shaming, but rather looking at things from the perspective of awareness.

I Am Aware

I Am Aware

I Am Aware

I Am Willing

I discover a willingness to more deeply

explore these ever-expanding patterns.

Soon the nuances appear. I notice

where things are similar,

and where they are separate.

Ah, the ability to entertain the idea of change. Willingness is so important in life in general, and especially when related to forgiveness. I think of it as putting yourself in the starting blocks of forgiveness. Are you willing to do so?

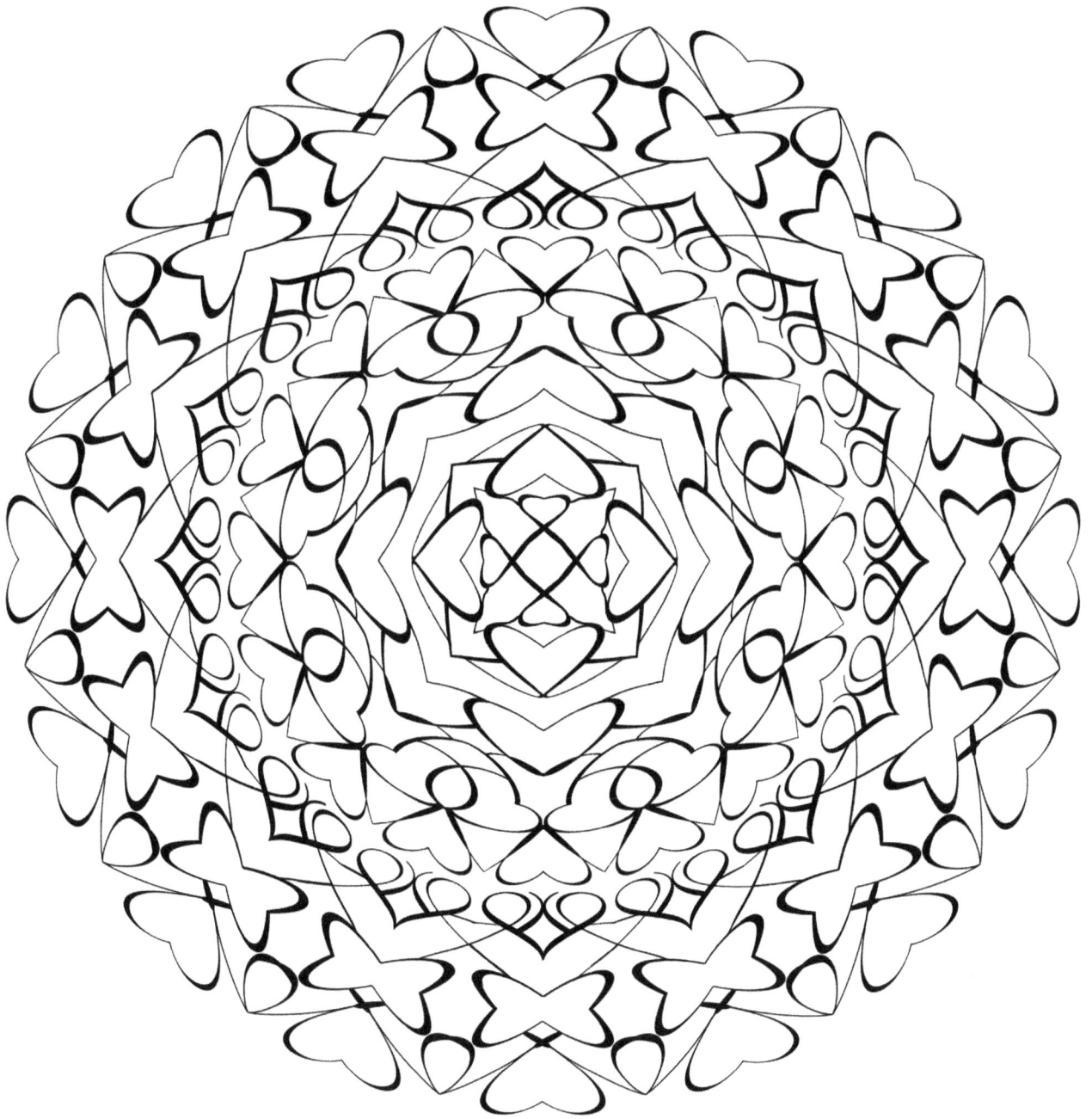

I Am Willing

I Am Willing

I Am Willing

I Am Trusting

From the dark, light begins to emerge.

I see things I've never seen before.

I feel things I've never felt before.

I'm beginning to trust.

I take a step in the direction of my dream.

Learning how to trust again is a big step forward in the forgiveness process. It may not come overnight, but you can get to a place of trusting others and yourself again.

I Am Trusting

I Am Trusting

I Am Trusting

I Am Taking Responsibility

As the light on my path increases,

shapes and colors start to make more sense.

I see my role, and the connections and

choices I freely make.

I feel more empowered than ever before.

The "R" word here is not about accepting responsibility for wrong doing (although you can if you want) but rather taking responsibility for yourself and the way you feel. Blaming and shaming will get you nowhere.

I Am Taking Responsibility

I Am Taking Responsibility

I Am Taking Responsibility

I Am Taking Action

Movement and choices bring freedom.

No longer sitting on the fence,

I make a bold decision to move.

Joy and freedom bring increased confidence.

You can get yourself on the proper path through forgiveness. It can mean choosing differently and consciously creating your life. Taking action can be one of the boldest things you ever do-and so worth it!

I Am Taking Action

I Am Taking Action

I Am Taking Action

_____

_____

_____

_____

_____

_____

_____

_____

_____

_____

_____

_____

_____

_____

_____

_____

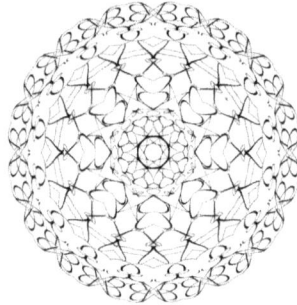

I Am Releasing

It's all starting to make sense now.

My path is becoming clearer and brighter.

I'm willing to notice where I can say, "yes"

to what is serving me, and where

I can say, "no" to what no longer does.

Many times the monkey mind of shame, guilt and limiting beliefs takes hold and keeps you in its grip for years. Look for opportunities to think differently and question what's not serving you in these areas.

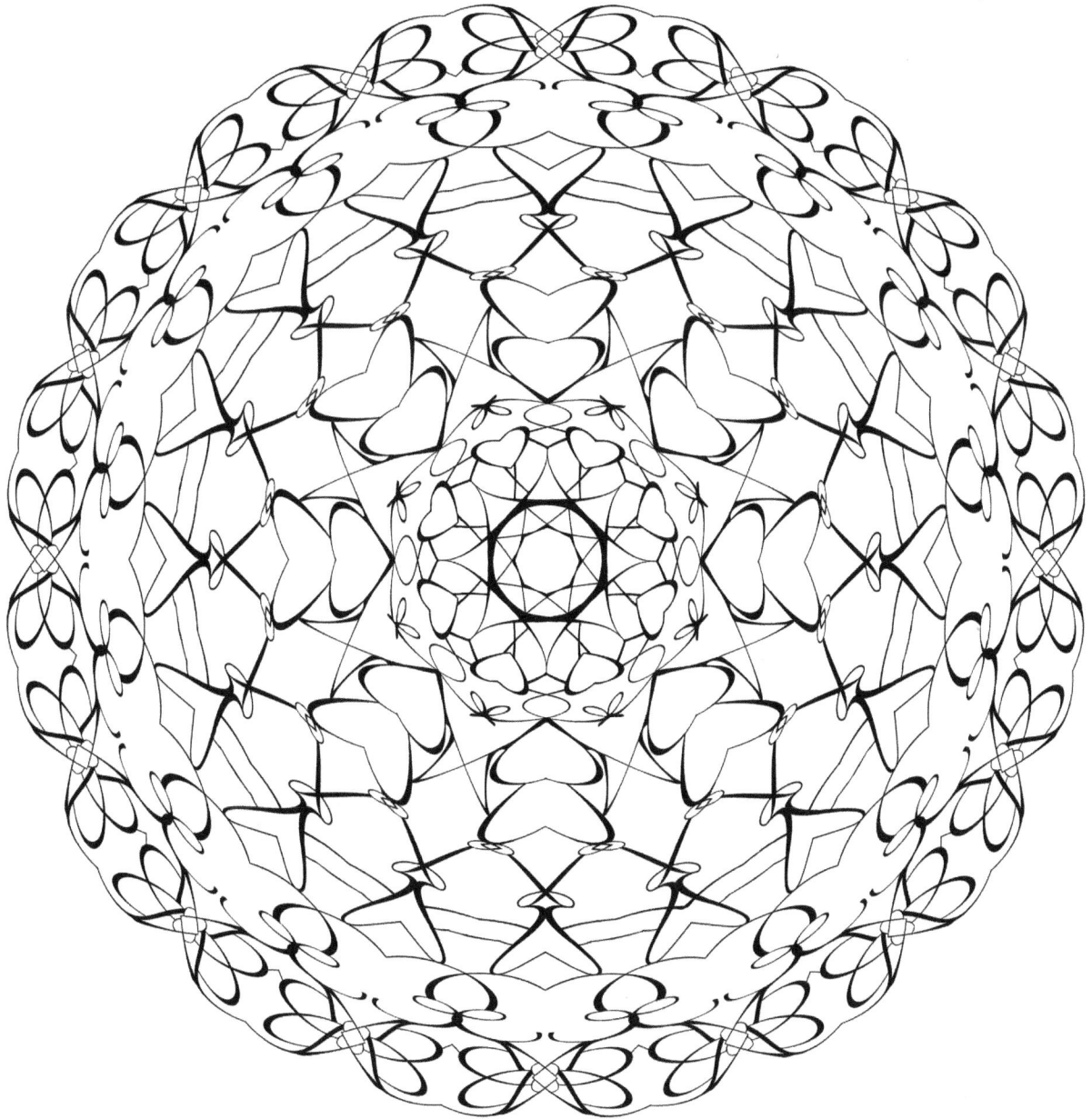

I Am Releasing

I Am Releasing

I Am Releasing

I Am Forgiving

I see more and more light, and

I'm beginning to feel more

freedom and peace within me.

I no longer allow behavior that

doesn't resonate for me. I set it free with love.

I accept all parts of me. The dark and the light. The behaviors, decisions and choices that got me here. It all makes me the beautiful being I am today. I allow understanding and compassion for myself and others to be who we are right now.

I Am Forgiving

I Am Forgiving

I Am Forgiving

I Am Grateful

On this journey of forgiveness,

I now see the colors and shapes

of my life from a different perspective.

Without needing to know exactly why things happened,

I allow myself to see it differently. I am grateful.

Gratitude is powerful. It creates the opportunity to change our perspectives from looking at our lives as sad or heavy and not worth anything to looking at them with meaning and purpose. It changes the story line.

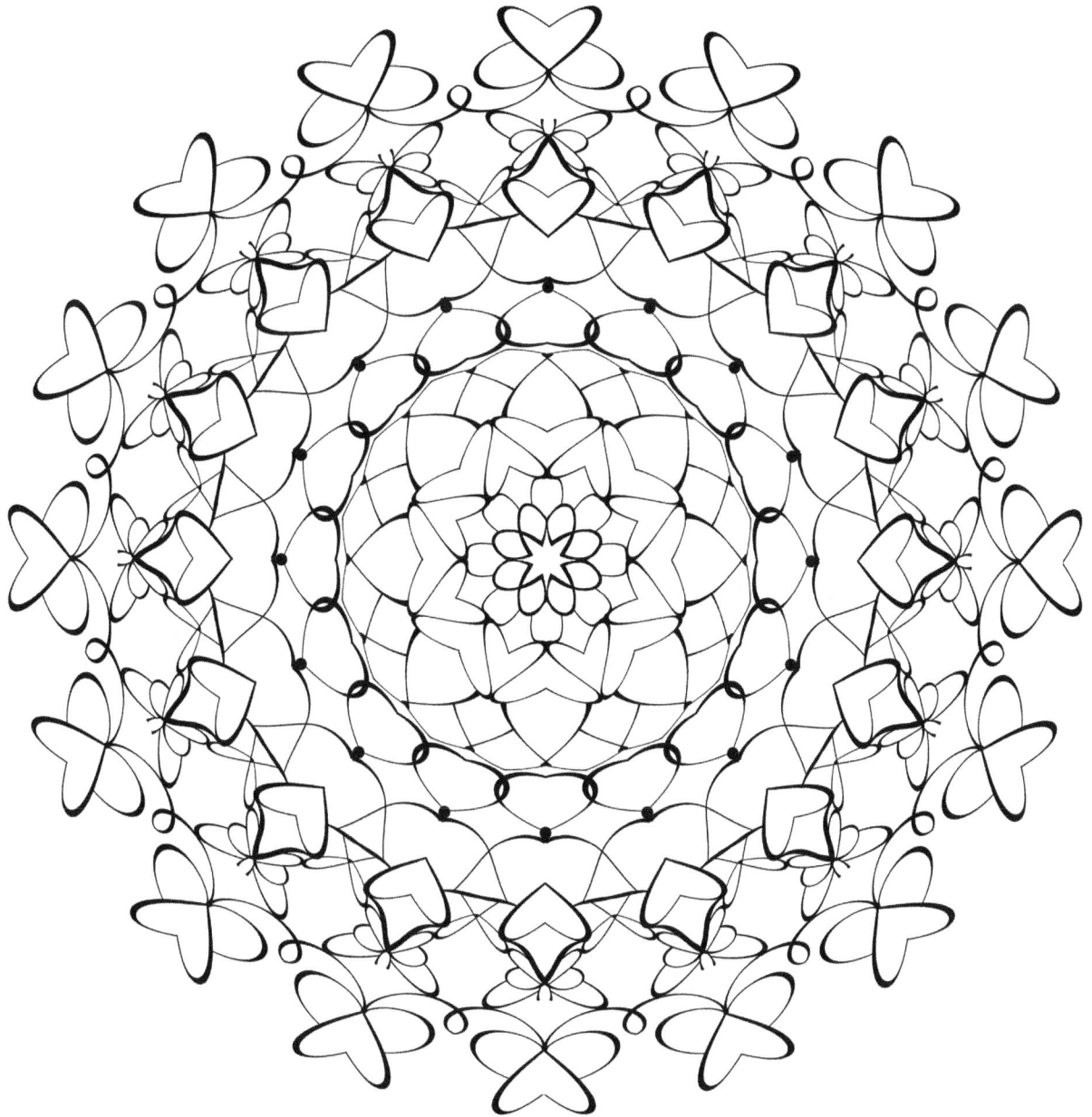

I Am Grateful

I Am Grateful

I Am Grateful

I Am Free

As I sink deeper into all that I have seen

and felt on this journey of forgiveness,

I see that freedom is right on the other side.

I release the ties that bind my mind and heart.

It's like flying without leaving the ground.

No longer heavy or chained to old stories or beliefs about how I need to be, I am releasing the "shoulds" and embracing the "coulds." I breathe with ease and grace. I feel a lightness in my body and mind. It feels like flowing water in a stream carving its own pathway to new beginnings.

I Am Free

I Am Free

I Am Free

About the Artist

Michelle Radomski
Publisher, Book Alchemist, Mandala Artist, and Bestselling Author

My Bio ... In five chapters:

Chapter One ... Who I Am
I'm Michelle. Happily married to My Love for 30 years. Proud mama of two powerful young women who are making their way (and making a difference) in this world. I love warm socks, new crayons, the magic of color, the power of words, and the truth that underneath it all **We Are Glorious.**

Chapter Two ... What I Do
I help authors, artists, writers, and other creative souls get brave, take action and finally, *finally* show up to be seen and heard. I offer a variety of opportunities and tools, (including start-to-finish publishing solutions) to ensure that your words and your work actually make their way out into the world. *Authentically. Bravely. For Real. Not someday. Not soon. Now.*

Chapter Three ... Why It Matters
In a word (or six) … **it matters because your voice matters.** You have a glorious gift to give. I know you do. The world needs it. I know it does. You also have a tender heart. The publishing world, the online world, and (let's face it) the world in general, can often feel too noisy, too big, and just *too much.* You need to publish your work in a way that feels honoring, authentic, and true. *That's what I do. Your voice is why I do it.*

Chapter Four ...What I Believe
This list could get long, long, long … so I picked my top three.
One, you are gifted and glorious beyond measure.
Two, if you hear a calling, it is because someone is placing the call. They need you to say yes.
Three, you have everything you need to answer the call. You just need to believe it.

Chapter Five ... What I Bring To Our Work Together
Three things. One, my personal journey from resistance to resilience. I know from my own experience that you *can* show up, fully and authentically, to your words and your work. *Two,* decades of immersion in the design and publishing world. *Three,* my heart, tenacity, and unwavering comittment to you and your voice.

Join my growing tribe of courageous authors, artists, writers, coaches, healers and other soul-filled creatives, I invite you to sign up for my newsletter, *Create Brave.* A few times a month I'll share encouragement, color, positivity, mandalas, creative showcases, and (sometimes) prezzies! Plus my tribe gets first dibs on every new publishing opportunity. **Reach out to me here (I'd love it):**
OneVoiceCan.com • 623-556-7967 • michelle@onevoicecan.com

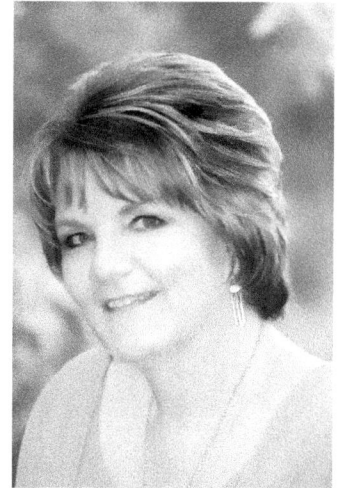

About the Author

Brenda Reiss
Forgiveness Coach

By sharing about myself and my work, I hope to give you comfort in knowing I can guide you through life's challenges.

First, allow me to share this simple perspective: each individual life is indeed a journey. And one of the biggest decisions each of us will ever make is how we wish to spend our life—as a victim, or as a victor.

Forgiveness is the key to restoring and maintaining well-being—forgiveness of ourselves, of others and even of life, itself. I guide others through the powerful process of forgiveness using several transformative tools and techniques. The forgiveness work forever changed me and I feel it is important to understand the depths from which I rose, inspiring the phoenix in my logo.

My "baggage car" began slowing my train of life down, early on—when I was abandoned at the age of three. This precipitated a life fraught with every imaginable form of abuse, from mental and physical to sexual, even spiritual in nature. This manifested into in eating disorders, addictions, toxic relationships and life-threatening health—among other challenges. I was resigned to a seemingly eternal culture of victimhood. I blamed anyone and everyone but myself.

But forgiveness has transitioned me from victim to victor. I studied and became certified in a number of intuitive, healing and recovery modalities—both traditional and untraditional. All of these were integral to becoming the kind of coach I wanted to be—one who truly helps others.

Yet, I didn't truly "come into my own" until I discovered the power of forgiveness.

Forgiveness gave me the knowledge, confidence and resources to fully embrace the concept of becoming master of my own fate, and moving beyond my scars and challenges—no matter how arduous. Forgiveness has given me the ability to assist others to step into their own power. I am deeply, genuinely honored and privileged to work with each individual who reaches out to me. By giving me an opportunity to assist you in letting go of your baggage and moving beyond your most ardent challenges, I achieve my life's purpose. *Let me help you begin finding and achieving yours.*

Brenda

Brenda Reiss

Get More of Brenda

BRENDA REISS
Forgiveness *Coaching*

Download the free eBook
"11 Steps to Forgiveness"

Discover the key steps to bring about more joy in life.

In this book you will find how to:

- Bring more joy and peace to life.
- Practice healing through forgiveness.
- Use proven tools and techniques for getting started today!

Get the free eBook at
www.BrendaReissCoaching.com